Diego the Bilingual Duck & Four Friends

Ready for Summer Fun!

by

VIOLA GRAYS-WILEY

Building Reading Fluency
Preschool – Grade 2 (English & Spanish)

DIEGO & His
Four Friends
Ready for Summer Fun!

Copyright

DEDICATION

*This book is dedicated
to beginning readers
EVERWHERE,
Preschool through Second Grade,
ESL, and Special Needs' students.
An EXCELLENT RESOURCE
For TEACHING SIGHT WORDS-
Bilingual Students & Families
Parents, Grandparents,
Teachers and STUDENTS!!!*

Hello, I'm DIEGO!

Hola, Soy DIEGO!

I can't wait to get in the water!

No puedo esperar para Meterme en el agua!

I have four friends.
Tengo cuatro amigos.

One, Two, Three, Four
Uno, Dos, Tres, Cuatro

I do not see my friends.

No veo a mi amigos.

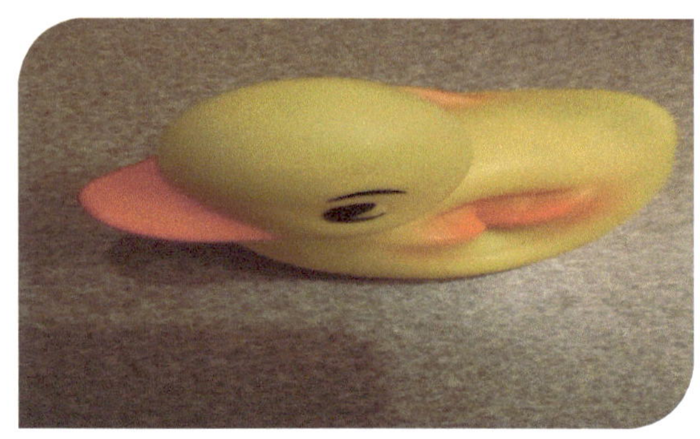

I am sad.

Estoy triste.

Can you help me find my friends?

Puedes ayudarme a encontrar a mis amigos?

Then I can be happy!
Entonces puedo ser feliz!

Look, I found one friend!

Mira, encontre una amigo!

Now, we can look for three more friends!

Ahora podemos buscar tres amigos mas!

Look, we found one more friend!

Mira, encontramos a uno amigo mas!

Now, we can look for two more friends.

Ahora, podemos buscar dos amigos mas.

Can you help me and my friends?

Puedes ayudarme a mi y a mi amigos?

Now, how many are we looking for?
One, Two, or Three?

Ahora cuantos buscamos ?
Uno, Dos, o Tres?

Did you say two more friends?

Dijiste dos amigos mas?

You are right!
Two more friends!

Tienes razon!
Dos amigos mas!

I can't wait to get in the water!

No puedo esperar para Meterme en el agua!

Look, we found one more friend!

Mira, tenemos uno amigo mas!

Now, how many friends do we need to find?

Ahora, cuantas amigos necesitamos encontrar?

Did you say one more?

Dijiste uno mas?

Yes, just one more friend!

Sis, solo uno amigo mas!

Look, we found one more friend!

Mira, encontramos a uno amigo mas!

I am so happy, I think
I am going to fly!

*Estoy tan feliz, que creo
que voy a volar!*

I found my four friends!

Encontre a mis cuatro amigos!

Now, I can get my boat!

Ahora puedo conseguir mi bote!

Are you ready for summer?

Estas lista para el verano?

I'm DIEGO and My Friends
and I are
Ready for SUMMER!

Soy, DIEGO, y mis amigos
y estoy lista para el verano!

Can you tell me what would be your best summer?

Puedes decrime cual
Seria tu mejor verano?

Summer Is Here!!!

El Verano Esta Aqui!

THE END